FINDING JESUS

Winston Rowntree

First published in Great Britain by Square Peg 2014

10

Copyright © Chris Ruddick 2014
Illustrations by Chris Ruddick
Jacket illustrations by Chris Ruddick
Jacket design by Tracey Winwood

Square Peg
Random House, 20 Vauxhall Bridge Road,
London SW1V 2SA

www.vintage-books.co.uk

Addresses for companies within The Random House Group Limited can be found at:
www.randomhouse.co.uk/offices.htm

The Random House Group Limited Reg. No. 954009

A CIP catalogue record for this book
is available from the British Library

ISBN 9780224101110

Printed and bound in China by C&C Offset Printing Co Ltd

When Jesus told his disciples, "I am with you always," most people assumed he was just adding a little figurative, feel-good flourish. As it turns out, Christ is a pretty literal guy. Whether you're rocking out at a concert, dancing at the club, or seeing a movie, our Savior is everywhere you go. Not in a creepy Police song way, per se, but more like a Godly wingman who knows how to appear and disappear on cue. All you need to know is where to look. But be prepared: the Son of God is sneaky. The whole conspicuous thing didn't work out so well last time around, so now he's decided to blend in with the crowd. Bearded hipster or God's right-hand man? Hard to tell. Robe-wearing hippie or the risen Lord out for a good time? Your guess is as good as anyone's. Still, if you look closely enough, somewhere in the blur of people J.C.'s waiting for you to spot him. While finding Jesus isn't necessarily easy, it's never been more fun.

ACKNOWLEDGMENTS

The author wishes to thank Suzanne O'Neill and everyone at Three Rivers Press for publishing this and for being such an unqualified joy to work with; Holly Schmidt and everyone at Hollan Publishing for the great book concept and representation; Jack O'Brien and Dan O'Brien and everyone at Cracked.com for a whole lot of stuff; and Anna, Mom and Dad, and everyone at The Family for the constant support and for being almost as proud of me as I am of them.